WORLDWIDE
STEAM
RAILWAYS

KEITH STRICKLAND
FOREWORD BY PAUL ATTERBURY

The
History
Press

Title page: Waiting for the signal to start, Ukraine, October 1994.

First published 2010

The History Press
The Mill, Brimscombe Port
Stroud, Gloucestershire, GL5 2QG
www.thehistorypress.co.uk

ISBN 978 0 7524 5156 5
Typesetting and origination by The History Press
Printed in Malta.

Contents

Foreword

The steam locomotive, that magnificent creation of the nineteenth century, was probably at the zenith of its powers in the 1930s. The second half of the twentieth century witnessed its decline and gradual disappearance from many national networks. However, in some of the more remote parts of the world it continued to thrive and even lingered on in mainline service well into the twenty-first century. As a result, generations of enthusiasts and photographers have trekked around the world to experience and record the end of steam. Naturally, most of these have concentrated on the locomotives themselves, either survivors from an earlier age or massive giants representing the final achievement of steam, often photographed in spectacular landscape settings.

I grew up in the last decades of mainline steam in Britain and, like many small boys of my era, I spent hours on railway station platforms writing down the names and numbers of passing locomotives. My childhood was mostly spent around south London, and so my notebooks are filled with those famous Southern classes, the 'King Arthurs', the 'Schools', the 'Lord Nelsons' and my favourites, those distinctive Bulleid Pacifics, the 'Battle of Britains', 'West Countrys' and 'Merchant Navys'. I rarely ventured into other regions, though I had a secret admiration for the GWR, developed through an early passion for Brunel. It was this that made me understand, as I grew older, that there was much more to railways than locomotives. Engineering and architecture took over in my head and in my imagination, as I discovered the extraordinary structural legacy of the Victorian railway age.

All my life I have been a perennial train traveller. Work, and pleasure, have taken me around most of the surviving British network and I have walked many miles along the routes of lines that have been lost. I have travelled by train in many parts of Europe, around Australia and occasionally in North America, but I have never been to those great centres of the railway world, India, South-East Asia and China. Over many years I have often been tempted by brochures, railway books and films but have never given in. I now regret it deeply as it is through the photographs of Keith Strickland that I see what I have missed. There are many famous railway photographers who have produced volumes of magnificent images, but somehow Keith is a bit different. His photographs certainly show steam locomotives at their romantic best in many exciting parts of the world, but they do much more than that. Many he has photographed are ancient, dirty veterans, relics of an age when railways changed the world and still carried the stamp of a period when imperialism and rampant industrial might ruled. Railways were one of the foundation stones for the modern world, spreading a global network of industrial development and exploitation, and all that that has come to represent. Railways changed lives beyond measure, bringing both great wealth and great poverty and the freedom to travel and transport freight over long distances came with a high price tag. Somehow, Keith's photographs seem to express all of that and at their heart is the knowledge, the certainty, that railways are about people: the passengers, the staff, those whose living depends on the railways and those who simply watch. And many of the watchers are children, as it has always been.

For this, and many other reasons, I am delighted to know that the proceeds from this book will help the Railway Children charity. Keith is a generous man and a great photographer and, as an enthusiast, I can share his particular vision of the railway world. Railway enthusiasm is universal and all children seem to enjoy trains but children should not need to have to lead their young lives in the dangerous and harsh surroundings of the modern railway. The charity Keith supports hopes to change that and for that reason I hope many people enjoy this wonderful book.

Paul Atterbury

Chengde, China, October 1997.

Railway Children

Railway Children is a UK-based charity supporting street children who live on or around railway stations in many countries. When children are abandoned, orphaned, abused or exploited, many run to the world's cities and try to survive with other children in similar circumstances to their own. These children are vulnerable at the best of times, but are particularly at risk in the first few hours and days when they are the prey of those who would exploit, abuse and corrupt them. Railway Children focuses its support, through over forty partner organisations in India, East Africa and the UK, on the children who have lost or run from adult contact, and aims to intervene as early as possible when children arrive in the cities. The railway station is an important initial contact point.

Deraa, Syria, September 2008.

The charity, through its partners, runs drop-in centres, emergency night shelters and platform schools, many with the assistance of the local railway authorities, and reaches about 25,000 children a year. It then seeks to reconcile the child with its family if that is possible and in the child's best interest – about a quarter of the children supported in 2008 were returned home – or find, with the child's participation, the best long-term development option available. The charity was founded in 1995 by David Maidment, a career railwayman, most of its trustees come from the UK railway industry and half its £2 million annual income comes from individuals and companies associated with Britain's railways. Keith Strickland, the author of this book, is the charity's Company Secretary.

Railway Children
Registered charity No. 1058991

Introduction

Let's be clear. No false pretences. This book is deliberately intended to be different. It's not in the usual format for the genre. First, all the photographs are in black and white, of which more anon. Second, it aims to depict the *environment* in which steam trains could be found in the late twentieth and early twenty-first centuries on real, as opposed to museum, railways in various parts of the world. True, some of the trains depicted were arranged specially for the enthusiast, but all are, or were, on workaday railways.

There are lots of pictures of steam engines, of course, and jolly good I hope you'll find them too. But there's also the setting – urban, rural and industrial. There's the associated paraphernalia: signals, signs and such like. There are stations and engine sheds. There are people; railway staff, locals and even fellow photographers. And there are children who are often fascinated, not to say puzzled, by the antics of the latter. All go to make up the experience of steam railways.

What really makes this book different, I hope, is the overseas setting. Not one photograph was taken in the UK, which as fellow pedants will know does not include the Isle of Man. As explained in previous books, in 1974 I embarked on a hobby to see as much as I could of the world's last steam trains in everyday use. As the years have gone by, the number of countries with real steam has declined. At the time of writing, China is the only country where steam has survived to any extent, and then only at industrial locations such as coalmines and steelworks. Who knows what steam, if any, will remain by the time this book is published?

Fortunately, all has not been lost. In some cases, as in the former East Germany, tourism has helped to secure the future of steam railways which, though increasingly dependent on leisure business, still work day-in day-out to serve the local populace.

In other parts of the world, the railway authorities cooperate from time to time with specialist groups and go to considerable lengths to recreate the steam scene of yesteryear. Of course, this doesn't come cheap. Just imagine the logistics of replicating an authentic 1960s train today. The locomotive and rolling stock have to be 'right', and the route has to be one over which such a train ran in the '60s. The cost of making this happen means that a goodly number of participants is needed to make such events viable.

The focus of this collection is, therefore, on steam trains which were working for real at the time the pictures were taken or which were authentic recreations of the past. With one exception, none of the photographs has previously been published.

When hunting steam abroad, I prefer to travel solo or with a like-minded friend or two – sometimes even with my wife! Groups aren't my first choice. That said, the necessity for and pleasure of group travel, particularly where specially chartered trains are concerned, are readily acknowledged. In the light of the friendships made on such trips, perhaps a measure of humble pie would not be amiss. So, apologies to those into whose field of vision I may have unwittingly strayed; and also to those on the receiving end of an 'Oi' having unknowingly ventured into mine.

But what of the medium? Why black and white? Purely personal preference is the honest answer. In part, this is because the steam locomotive seems to lend itself to monochrome photography. It may also have something to do with nostalgia for an era which ended in Britain a long time ago. Whatever the reason, I started serious photography in black and white more years ago than I care to remember and no doubt will continue to do so until the last thud of the shutter.

Ah, thud? Yes. Every one of the photographs in this book was taken on a Pentax or Nikon manual SLR camera, with Ilford 35mm film. As long as these cameras continue to work, I'll go on using them. This isn't because of being pro-film or anti-digital, the arguments about which tend to go over my head. It's simply a matter of familiarity and comfort. Old-fashioned? At an age to be the proud possessor of a senior rail card, who cares? Mind you, once the negatives have been produced, they are scanned and stored on a PC. The days of the darkroom are over!

Among the countless people at home and abroad who have helped in my travels, three have been especially good friends – Brian Hammond, Graham Morfoot and Richard Turkington. Coming to terms with the digital age has been greatly aided by a best pal from school days, Tony Bagwell. But most importantly, huge thanks are due to my wife, Mary, who has heard the phrase, 'I must go to so-and-so before it's too late,' more times than I care to admit and who first encouraged me to do something useful with my photographic collection.

Finally, a word about the Railway Children, to which the royalties from the sale of this book are being donated. For me, railway stations are places of excitement. For thousands of children around the world, they are places of refuge, of despair and of personal danger; but with the help of the Railway Children they can become places of hope. After a lifetime of enjoying trains, there can be no better way of giving something back than by supporting this charity in its work with children who live on or around stations. Do please read the preface which the trustees' chairman has kindly contributed to this book, and take a moment to visit the website www. railwaychildren.org.uk. Better still, why not consider becoming a regular donor?

One reviewer of my *Steam Railways Around the World* said that the book revealed a personality which was 'enchanted by steam without being obsessed by it.' I liked that. I hope this book, too, conveys something of that enchantment. So, as someone once remarked, 'Hallelujah, and damn the diesels!'

Keith Strickland
Trowbridge, Wilts.
April 2010

1

People

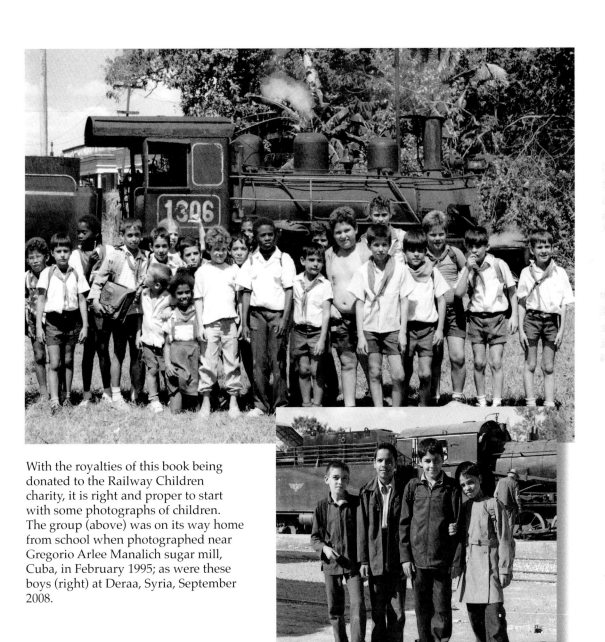

With the royalties of this book being donated to the Railway Children charity, it is right and proper to start with some photographs of children. The group (above) was on its way home from school when photographed near Gregorio Arlee Manalich sugar mill, Cuba, in February 1995; as were these boys (right) at Deraa, Syria, September 2008.

Left: Children the world over love to have their picture taken as evidenced here in this photo taken at Mafrag, Jordan, in September 2008.

Right: Orlovat, Serbia, June 2008.

Right: Sir
Lowry's Pass,
a station in
Cape Province,
South Africa, is
photographed
here in July
1995. On a line
which normally
saw only
freight traffic, a
passenger train
was a rare event,
especially one
hauled by steam.

Opposite bottom: A game of hide and seek was being played by boys outside the sheds which served the railway system at Simon Bolivar sugar mill, Cuba, March 1995. No. 1363 was a 2–8–0 built by the Baldwin Locomotive Company, USA, in 1917.

Left: Families also love to pose, as seen here at Polgahawela Junction, Sri Lanka, February 1994.

Below left: Tatkon, Burma, January 2007.

Below right: Pingdingshan, China, October 2007.

Left: A shunter at Daban, China, with his flags in March 2004. He doesn't look very happy, but who would working in a temperature of -20 degrees Celsius?

Right: On long-distance trains in China, each carriage has its own lady attendant. The *Jingpeng China Orient Express* is seen here in March 2004.

Two proud people. The Pathan tribesman (left) just happened to come along as we were waiting by the side of the narrow gauge line from Kohat to Thal, Pakistan, in February 1988. My taxi driver (right) in Delhi, photographed in December 1998, clearly wanted his picture taken. Behind him is the oldest working steam locomotive in India which is occasionally used on special trains. Named *Fairy Queen*, she was built for the East Indian Railway by the firm of Kitson in Leeds as long ago as 1855. I wonder how many of the original parts survive?

Above left and right:
Footplate crew. Those on the left wait to leave Wolsztyn, Poland with a passenger train for Poznan in April 1994. In the right-hand photograph, the driver and fireman pose at Indwe, South Africa, in July 1995, while working the 'Drakensberg Farewell Railtour' over the Maclear branch. It was no surprise that the gentleman with the beard was nicknamed Castro.

There's mention later on of my experiences driving steam trains in Poland. These two gentlemen were the crew under whose tutelage I drove my first train in April 1999. Having scrubbed up, they were relaxing outside the sheds at Wolsztyn. Judging by their smiles, I can't have done too badly, or were they smiling *at* me?

Gangers take a break from their work in Sri Lanka as a special train from Badulla to Kandy passes in February 1994. No. 340 *Frederick North* is a 4–6–0 built in Darlington by the firm of Robert Stephenson & Hawthorn in the mid 1940s. Banking the rear of the train is no. 213, a 4–6–0 tender-tank locomotive constructed by the Vulcan Foundry at Newton-le-Willows in 1922.

'Gricer. Noun, British, informal. A trainspotter. Origin uncertain. Perhaps a humorous representation of . . . grouser.' So says the dictionary. Most who regard themselves as gricers would probably take issue with the reference to trainspotting, which implies no more than the collecting of numbers. As to grousing, I suppose like anglers we are prone to moan about the one that got away. There's also the need for endless patience. How many hours have we spent waiting for the perfect conditions for that master photograph?

Above left: As the shadows lengthen and the temperature dips below zero, these gricers are still waiting for the next steam-hauled freight to appear near Shina, China, in November 1996. *Right:* For this poor fellow, the waiting was just too much. Chengde, China, October 1997.

Below left: Mr Zhou, seen here in October 2007, is a rare Chinese gricer. He was in contact by mobile phone with the crews of the steam-hauled freights on the Yankuang coal railway and could therefore ensure lots of black smoke at the required location. After a day's photography, he kindly entertained us in his apartment next to the railway workshops where he was a manager. The highlight was his wife's singing dog – but that's another story. *Right:* Here is proof of the lengths to which some photographers will go to get the best shot. Pretoriuskloof, South Africa, July 1995.

Above left: When there's nothing else to do, relax. Here is a happy group on the train from Beijing to Datong, China, in November 1982. *Right:* After riding the early morning steam-hauled passenger train from Baiyin, it's time for coffee and a chat with the friendly loco crew at Shenbutong, China, in March 2009. Through our Chinese guide Alan (far left), we discovered that the station, which served the local copper mines, was supposed to be out-of-bounds to foreigners. The author's camera bag and the ubiquitous (for China) flask of hot water are evident. *Below:* By the hotel pool at Santa Clara, Cuba, in March 1995. The bus which was to take us to our next sugar mill had broken down so it was time for a cocktail and a cigar.

Left: As my wife has often said, she's been to some pretty un-touristy places as a result of my hobby. With local guide Nancy (on the right), we visited the Dahuichang limestone railway near Beijing, China, on a bitterly cold day in December 2000.

Below: Zhou Yang was the guide for a group tour in China in November 1996. During a very long wait for the expected train, the crossing-keeper near Basuo on tropical Hainan Island took pity on Zhou and brought out a chair. Sadly, by the time the train came, the light had gone. In the meantime, a different type of motive power provided some interest.

The delights of India's hill railways have been appreciated by gricers for a long time. In the last years of the twentieth century, the 2ft gauge line to Darjeeling had something of a hand-to-mouth existence. Often closed because of landslides, political difficulties or shortages of coal, it seemed the line's days were doomed. In the late 1990s, the Darjeeling Himalayan Railway Society was formed in the UK with the aim of lobbying the powers-that-be to secure the railway's future by developing its tourist potential. With the encouragement of the society, the Indian authorities and other local organisations have taken up the challenge to such an extent that the railway is now a World Heritage Site. I was pleased when this photograph was used on the front cover of the society's very first magazine. It shows a train at Tindharia with loco no. 779, which at that time carried the name *Mountaineer*, in December 1985. British-built, she is a veteran of the 1890s. I had no idea the children were in the frame until the film was developed – serendipity, indeed.

2

Narrow Gauge

What is narrow gauge? If standard gauge is 4ft 8½in, anything greater must logically be broad, and anything less narrow. By this definition, the 3ft 6in railways of South Africa are narrow in gauge, but few would regard them as narrow in character given the height, width and overall size of their locomotives and rolling stock. Applying this test of scale to the metre gauge is more problematic. The networks of the Indian sub-continent were of mainline proportions, yet in other parts of the world metre gauge lines definitely had the narrow feel about them.

In Syria the remnant of a line which long ago ran to Beirut still operates out of the suburbs of Damascus, though now only for trippers. Built in 1895, it has the unusual gauge of 1.05 metres. Loco no. 755, a 2–6–0 constructed in Switzerland for the opening of the railway, takes a Railway Touring Company special to Fidjeh in September 2008.

Class WD 2–8–2 no. 1567 shunts on the metre gauge at Agra, India, while a tiffin wallah passes by, in November 1985.

The Harz Mountains in what used to be East Germany have an extensive metre gauge network of lines which survived long enough after German unification to be transferred into private ownership. It was, and to some extent still is, operated as two distinct systems. Alexisbad is a junction on what was the Selketalbahn where Mallett 0–4–4–0 tank no. 99 5906-5 takes water before working a passenger train to Gernrode in May 1986.

Two narrow gauge railways near Germany's Baltic Sea coast also survived into the post-communist era to be run by private companies. The line from Bad Doberan to Kuhlungsborn has a 90cm gauge. Its best known feature is the street running in the town of Bad Doberan. Seen here in April 2003, 2–8–2 tank no. 99 2321-0 pauses in the middle of the street at one of the town's 'train-stops'.

Sister loco no. 99 2322-8 emerges from Bad Doberan's main shopping street in April 2003 and heads across a main road. There used to be no traffic lights.

Rugen is Germany's largest island. At one time, it had a 75cm gauge light railway with routes totalling some 60 miles. A part of this survives, though now predominantly providing a service for tourists and holiday-makers. In April 2003, 2–8–0 tank no. 99 4802 waits to leave the eastern terminus at Gohren.

At Binz, no. 99 4802 waits with a train from Putbus to Gohren while 0–8–0 tank no. 53 rolls into the station, heading in the opposite direction, in April 2003. She was built in 1925 by Vulcan in what is now the Polish city of Szczecin, but which was then Stettin in Germany.

A number of 75cm gauge railways with daily traffic remain within striking distance of Dresden in the south-east of Germany. One of these runs from Radebeul to Radeburg. Level crossing shots are tricky and nerve-wracking as there's always the chance some inconsiderate driver will block the view at the last minute. All's well at Moritzburg in October 2004 as 0–10–0 tank no. 99 713 leaves with a train for Radeburg.

The charm of the narrow gauge is illustrated here by no. 99 713 again, near Barnsdorf, Germany, in October 2004.

In neighbouring Poland, a few narrow gauge lines also managed to hang on into the twenty-first century and the one from Gneizno still saw the occasional freight. More excitingly, it was possible to hire one's own train and, once out of the town, to drive it! The 'Strickland Special' pauses in October 2001 while crew and passengers shop for lunch at the local store.

Later, one of the party takes the regulator as the small but perfectly formed no. 1785 storms across an unguarded level crossing. Class Px48 was a Polish design which became standard on the country's 75cm lines.

Continuing the European theme, here is a specially chartered train near Eichberg on the 76cm gauge Waldviertalbahn in Austria . . .

. . . and later near Alt Weitra in October 2004.

For much of its 30 or so miles, the 76cm gauge Ybbstalbahn follows the course of a lovely valley in the Austrian Alps. Here, 0–6–4 no. 598.02 leaves Grosshollenstein with a specially chartered train.

This loco, photographed in October 2004, may be small, but she can still make a lot of smoke.

The Czech Republic and Hungary have narrow gauge lines which still provide a daily service for the local community. Apart from having an unpronounceable name, Jindrichuv Hradec is the terminus of two 76cm gauge lines which since 1998 have been run by a private company. By all accounts they are thriving and while diesels work the regular trains, steam is kept for specials. No. U37.002 is a 0–6–2 tank built by Krauss in the city of Linz as long ago as 1898. She rests at Kamenice nad Lipou in October 2004 with a photographic charter while participants enjoy a lunch of goulash and wonderful Czech beer in a nearby restaurant.

It's almost sunset by the time the special completes the journey to the northern terminus at Obratan.

In Hungary in April 2001, no. 490.053 performs a run-past with a special from Kecskemet to Bugac on a 76cm gauge line which, at the time, saw just three return trains a day.

And so, eventually, to China whose far north-east once had a goodly number of narrow gauge lines, most of which were developed for forestry. That at Huanan owes its survival to coal mines at Hongguang 30 miles away. Seen here in February 2004, 0–8–0 no. 044 heads a train of empties across a bleak landscape (above and left) while no. 004 (below) simmers outside the sheds at Huanan.

Something very special indeed. Steam railcar no. 331, constructed by the Sentinel Wagon Works, Shrewsbury, in 1928 for use on the 2ft 6in Kelani Valley line in what was then Ceylon. Restored to working order in 1990, it looked superb in a livery of deepish red with yellow lining. At the time, no. 331 was believed to be the only steam-powered Sentinel railcar at work in the world. She is seen at Narahenpita on mixed gauge track in February 1994.

To return to the question posed at the beginning of this chapter, if the strict definition of narrow gauge is anything less than 4ft 8½in, the Mount Washington Cog Railway in New Hampshire, USA, must count as narrow even though its gauge is 4ft 8in. The railway is obviously for tourists but as it's been taking passengers to the summit of Mount Washington since 1869, it probably now counts as 'real'. In less than 3 miles, the line rises 3,600ft. It's a mighty steep climb and, sound-wise, a volcanic one. *Great Gulf* descends to Marshfield Base Station with its single carriage in August 1994.

3

Stations

Above: Port Soderick, Isle of Man, April 1996.

Right: There's a bit of cheating on this page because, as Kingston is at the end of a preserved line in New Zealand, it's not a workaday railway (see my *Steam Through Five Continents*). That said, this photograph, taken in October 1991, demonstrates that in some parts of the world there's no such thing as a printed timetable for the public. Train times are simply chalked on a board.

Right: Sometimes there isn't a shelter for intending passengers and the only access is a footpath across fields. This 'station', seen in April 1996, serves the Isle of Man's airport, though no doubt more in theory than in practice.

In the 1990s, the line from Caledon to Cape Town, South Africa, still carried regular freight traffic. This was especially so in the apple-picking season when train loads of fruit were railed to Cape Town docks for export. Class GO Garratt no. 2575 leaves Elgin in July 1995 with the re-creation of a mixed train – i.e. a train conveying passengers as well as freight. With a 4–8–2 + 2–8–4 wheel arrangement, she is a truly mighty machine for a railway with a gauge of 3ft 6in. No. 2575 was built in 1954 by Henschel.

Opposite top: The Hedjaz railway was built in the first years of the twentieth century, primarily to take pilgrims south from Damascus towards Mecca in what is now Saudi Arabia. The southernmost part was never completed for its full intended length, and what was built became the target of Lawrence of Arabia's escapades during the First World War when he was helping the local Arabs to overthrow their Turkish rulers. Between Damascus and Amman, the capitals of present-day Syria and Jordan, there are no regular trains – neither passenger nor freight. What traffic there is seems to consist solely of special charters. Seen in September 2008, no. 85 makes a noisy departure from Amman with a special bound for Syria. The crane on the right is a reminder of how important local goods traffic used to be on our railways. There was a time when even the smallest station had its own goods yard, or at least a loading bay, complete with crane, weighing machine and, most probably, cattle pens.

Opposite bottom: Travellers making the through journey between the two countries change trains and locos at Deraa, just on the Syrian side of the border. In September 2008, no. 85 of the Jordanian Railways runs round the train which it has just brought in from Amman while Syrian Railways no. 91 rests at the adjacent platform. The former is a Pacific built in Japan in the 1950s. The latter, a 2–8–0, is much older having been supplied to the original Hedjaz railway.

At the other end of the scale, size-wise, this diminutive 0–6–2 tank ran on the 2ft 6in gauge light railway from Futwa to Islampur in northern India. She was constructed in 1919 by the Leeds firm of Manning Wardle. She waits to leave Futwa in November 1985 with a passenger train of somewhat decrepit carriages. Indeed, someone remarked that they looked like cattle wagons. However, out of sight at the rear was the directors' saloon. Though having seen far better days, this at least had glass in the windows. It also had a coal-fired stove on which to brew *chai*, essential for any Indian journey.

The Jiayang Colliery Railway (commonly known as the Shibanxi line) in Sichuan Province, southern China, was built in 1958 to carry coal from mines to a power station. The busiest part is electrified, but steam-hauled passenger and freight trains still serve hill communities which have no roads to the outside world. Everything, including livestock, is carried by rail. Recently the line has started to be promoted as a tourist attraction but essentially it remains a lifeline for the local population. Villagers wait for an 'up' afternoon train as it arrives at Yue Jin in October 2007.

The terminus at Sroda, Poland, in April 1994, with an afternoon train from Zaniemysl arriving behind no. 1726. This line has since closed to regular traffic.

The fire brigade is often the only source of water at stations where the arrival of a steam train is a rare event. This photograph was taken at Despotovac, Serbia, in June 2008.

In the first years of the twenty-first century, it was truly amazing that steam locos could be found at work on a daily basis on a national network in Europe. It was even more surprising that complete amateurs were allowed to drive them. But that's exactly what happened at Wolsztyn, Poland, and hopefully continues to happen at the time this book is published. The Wolsztyn Experience is run by an ex-pat who brokered a business arrangement with the Polish railway authorities to allow people like me to drive steam locomotives on scheduled passenger trains and, until they ceased to run, on freights – under the supervision of the normal crew, of course. The income which this brought to the business helped to defray the cost of maintaining the locos based at the Wolsztyn depot. The most handsome of the fleet was this Pacific which has just arrived at Wolsztyn station, a typical communist-era utilitarian structure, with a train from Leszno in April 1999. I have driven this loco and on one occasion reached the metric equivalent of 60mph. 'Thrilling' seems such an inadequate description!

For me, the most enjoyable driving turn was the first train of the day to Zbaszynek which left Wolsztyn at 4.30 a.m. or thereabouts, returning two hours later with early morning commuters. There was quite a steep climb out of Wolsztyn. The sensation of being in control as the loco barked its way up the bank in the pre-dawn blackness was indescribable. It really was pure magic. A few years previously, in April 1994, Class Ol49 no. 81 waits to leave Wolsztyn with a train of double-decker stock which at that time was scheduled to depart at 4.49 a.m. The only passenger appears to be the guard. With a 2–6–2 wheel arrangement, the Ol49s were a post-war class designed for passenger work on secondary routes.

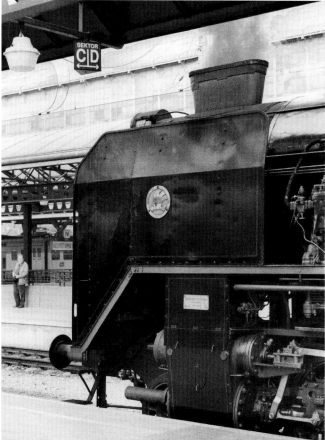

There's a style of communist-era architecture which survives throughout the former Eastern Bloc countries; drab, austere and soulless are three adjectives which come to mind, so let's talk about the locomotive instead. Seen here in Tokad, Hungary, in May 2001, 4–4–0 no. 204 is a lone example of a once-numerous class. Over 200 locos of this type were built in Budapest between 1881 and 1905 intended for express passenger work. Withdrawn in 1952, no. 204 was restored to working order in 1988.

It's obvious this photograph wasn't taken to show the architectural delights of one of Prague's main stations, Hlvani. The front end of no. 534.0323 looks impressive as she waits to leave with a train for Davle in September 1995. With a 2–10–0 wheel arrangement, over 500 locos of this class were constructed between 1945 and 1957. The emblem on the smoke deflector indicates this one was built by Skoda.

Steam locomotives obviously need to take on fresh supplies of water at frequent intervals. Prominent here is the tower which feeds the water cranes from which Class CWD 2–8–2 no. 5085 is being replenished during the course of a journey from Samasata to Bahawalnagar, Pakistan, in February 1988. This locomotive, built in 1945, was one of 800 supplied by American and Canadian manufacturers during and after the Second World War to cope with an enormous increase in traffic on Indian railways.

No. 99 713 on a photographers' charter, waits to cross the regular passenger train at Moritzburg on the 75cm gauge line from Radebeul to Radeburg in October 2004. She is a survivor from a class of forty-seven locos built between 1923 and 1927 to a design of what was then the Saxon State Railway. The village of Moritzburg is locally famous for its eighteenth-century hunting palace. This connection may account for the antlers on the station building.

No. 490.053 arrives at Bugac with a passenger train on the narrow gauge line from Kecskemet to Kiskunmajsa, Hungary, in April 2001. First introduced in 1905, locos of this class continued to be built until 1950; this example emerged from the workshops in 1942.

On the Waldviertalbahn in Austria in October 2004, no. 399.04 arrives at the station of Alt Weitra. Owned by the state railways, the line from Gmund to Gross Gerungs was modernised in the late 1980s with the introduction of railcars and a speeded-up service. Despite this, passenger numbers declined and trains were withdrawn in 2001. Since then, the line has seen frequent specials such as this one organised by the UK operator Steam Loco Safari Tours.

The top left corner of Slovenia is occupied by the south-eastern extremities of the Alps. Through this area runs a highly scenic single-track line from Jesenice via Bled to Nova Goria on the Italian border and bridges and tunnels abound. Set in a narrow valley among wooded hills, Podbrdo is at the western end of the longest of the tunnels. No. 25.026 (built in 1920) arrives with a train of vintage carriages bound for Bled in June 2008.

Opposite top: After arriving at Victoria Falls in the late afternoon with a freight from Thomson Junction, Class 15 Garratt no. 377 pulls the stock of the overnight train to Bulawayo into the station where some of the intending passengers have already gathered in July 1989. This class of loco carried the names of species of native wildlife. No. 377 was named *Udwai*, the local term for the Secretary Bird. With a 4–6–4 + 4–6–4 wheel arrangement, this loco was built by Beyer Peacock in 1948. In the late 1980s, the lines radiating from Bulawayo were *the* place to experience Garratts at work on both freight and passenger trains. More can be seen in my book *Steam Railways Around the World*.

Opposite bottom: In a chapter on stations, one might expect some comment on architecture. The British had a habit of providing fort-like stations in the tribal areas of what is now Pakistan, hence the crenellations at Laki Marwat Junction on the 2ft 6in gauge line from Mari Indus. That's enough about buildings. Of much more interest is this delightful 2–8–2 loco, seen here in February 1988, built in Glasgow by the North British Locomotive Co. in 1921.

There's much in this February 1994 scene which betrays the colonial origins of the railways of Sri Lanka: the water crane, signal, telegraph poles (a long-gone feature of the British landscape) and the engine itself, *Frederick North*, which has already appeared in the first chapter. The banana plants (behind the signal) and the Buddhist stupa (on the hillside above the cab) are clues to the tropical setting of Hatton, Sri Lanka.

Was the architect of this mock-Tudor signal-box in Bago, Burma (seen in January 2007), homesick for England?

This station carried marks of the fighting which plagued the Balkans in the early 1990s. The lady is standing on what passes for a platform in Ljubace, Bosnia-Herzegovina, in June 2008.

Pretty well every station, however humble, has a name-board. Pretoriuskloof was on the southern approaches to the Lootsberg Pass in South Africa. The name is glimpsed through the gap between the wheels and the boiler of a locomotive which had stopped at the station with a north bound train in July 1995.

4

Passenger Trains

Let's start with some real passenger trains. It's difficult to write with certainty about the remaining steam operations in China. The authorities claimed they would eliminate steam before the 2008 Olympic Games but that didn't happen. Steam survived to a surprising extent in a number of industrial locations, but for how much longer is anyone's guess. Maybe it will all be gone by the time this book sees the light of day. One can only comment on the situation on the ground at the time of one's visit. The Teifa Mining Administration is situated in the north of the country. Linking coal mines with the national rail network is a 'private' system comprising four lines radiating from Daobingshan with an aggregate length of over 100 kilometres. All carry both passenger and freight traffic. In 2004 the system was 100 per cent steam using Class SY 2–8–2s and one Class JS 2–8–2. With approximately thirty timetabled trains a day, this was the last intensive steam passenger service on a normal workaday railway anywhere in the world. SY nos 1751 and 860 are seen at Daobingshan station in February 2004.

In sub-zero temperatures, the afternoon train from Yebaishou to Chifeng has just left the station at Shina, China, in this photograph from November 1996. The sight of a mainline steam-hauled passenger train working day-in day-out is one we shall never see again, more's the pity.

South Africa has long been a favourite destination for steam photographers because of its magnificent locomotives and its equally magnificent scenery. A visit in the late 1970s produced hundreds of locos but steam finished on the national network in 1992. Fortunately, the authorities were happy to cooperate with charter groups by providing locos and stock to recreate bygone scenes and so was born the steam photo safari. One such was the 'Drakensberg Farewell Railtour' organised by the UK operator Steam & Safaris. For two weeks in July 1995 this covered a huge chunk of South Africa, starting at Bloemfontein and finishing at Cape Town. The train was home for the whole of the time. We lived, ate and slept on it – a most agreeable and comfortable experience. Class 24 2–8–4 no. 3635 and Class 19D 4–8–2 no. 2698 double-head the train on the Maclear branch en route to Elliot. Both classes were designed for mixed traffic and were used extensively on all types of work. The Class 24 locos were manufactured by the North British Locomotive Co. in the late 1940s. No. 2698 came from the German makers Borsig a decade earlier.

Early morning on the branch line from Springfontein to Fauresmith with no. 2698.

At Fauresmith, the railway ran slap bang through the middle of the High Street. Goodness knows what the local shopkeepers thought of all that smoke!

The Class 25NC 2–10–2s were massive machines for a gauge of 3ft 6in. No. 3410 *Paula* was a North British product of the early 1950s. She is seen leaving Elstrow, south of Springfontein.

The next day *Paula* makes a vigorous departure from Petrusberg on the secondary mainline from Bloemfontein to Kimberley . . .

. . . and later returns, near De Brug. Poles and wires are often a nuisance for railway photographers but sometimes can be used to good effect in a composition.

The Lootsberg is, or was, a famous pass on a secondary line which in years gone by saw through trains between Johannesburg and Port Elizabeth. In a recreation of those days, two class 19Ds (no. 2698 at the front and no. 3324 at the rear) struggle up the last few yards on the approach to the summit from the north.

South Africa and neighbouring Zimbabwe were major users of Garratts, a design well-suited for heavy loads over steep and twisting gradients. My first experience of these mighty locos was in the late 1970s on the daily Cape Town to Port Elizabeth train which was worked by a Garratt for part of the route, including the Montagu Pass between George and Oudtshoorn. Approaching the pass from the north, Class GMAM no. 4072 tackles the climb in fine style with the 'Drakensberg Farewell Railtour' near Oupad. She has a 4–8–2 + 2–8–4 wheel arrangement.

Next day, she nears the summit on the climb from the south with its severe gradients and curves. South African Railways used both British and German builders when ordering the class GMAMs. No. 4072 came from Henschel in the early 1950s.

Opposite: Ukraine was another country offering live-in train safaris, although the standard of sleeping accommodation didn't match that of South Africa. Food and drink were also rather different. No. 20.2714 is a class FD 2–10–2, seen here between Lamolintzy and Kadievka in September 1994. In the ten years from 1931, the USSR built more than 3,000 locos of this class which became one of the pre-war Soviet standard freight designs. The class was one of several to be named after political worthies, FD being the initials of Felix Dzerzhinsky (1877–1926), the founder of the Soviet secret service. In the late 1950s, 2,000 FDs were sold to China where they were converted from the Russian gauge of 5ft to standard gauge and termed the Friendship class. I remember seeing a few on my first visit to China in 1982.

Above: Another USSR freight design was class SO (CO in the Cyrillic alphabet) named after Sergo Ordzhonikidze (1886–1937), a close friend of Stalin and who, at the time of his death, was Commissar of Heavy Industry in the Politburo. As far as anyone knows, nearly 2,000 locos of this 2–10–0 class were built between 1935 and 1941. No. 17.4371 is seen en route from Pukov to Berezovitza, Ukraine, in September 1994.

I'm not a lover of glint shots but will occasionally have a go to see what the results are like. Here is no. 17.4371 near Berezovitza, Ukraine, in September 1994.

Pacific class 16DA no. 876 near Thaba Nchu, South Africa, July 1995.

Neither am I a great fan of bridges and viaducts though they can add interest to a composition as here. Class Ty3 no. 2 heads a specially chartered train from Wolsztyn to Konotop, Poland, in April 1994.

Sixty of the Class 477 tank locomotives were built for the Czech railways in the early 1950s. With their high-pitched boilers, these machines had a very impressive appearance. Painted light blue with red wheels, they were knicknamed *papousek* (parrot) by the local crews because of the bright colours. No. 477.043 is seen near Hyskov on a passenger train from Beroun to Rakovnik in October 2002.

Somewhere in Syria, September 2008, sees no. 262, a 2–8–2 built by the German firm Hartmann in 1918, with a Railway Touring Company (RTC) special of very dilapidated carriages. The wives among the group were not amused.

In Jordan, no. 23 heads another special in the suburbs of Amman. Of obvious British appearance, she was built by the firm Robert Stephenson & Hawthorn in 1951.

Pacific no. 629 heads a RTC special north of Bago bound for Mandalay, Burma, in January 2007. What an elegant engine. Unsurprisingly, she hails from Britain whose designers seemed to place more emphasis on graceful lines than did their counterparts abroad. The young men are scooping sand from the river bed.

No. 629 later on the same train, also in January 2007. From a photographic point of view, the vegetation showing above the train's roof-line is a bit of a distraction. On the plus side, the signal adds interest to a scene which may prove to be unrepeatable because in 2008 the Burmese railway authorities suddenly withdrew from service all their remaining steam locos. Whether any will ever emerge to run again remains to be seen.

The specialist tour operation Steam Loco Safari Tours (SLST) is run by a photographer who goes to great lengths to re-create authentic scenes of yesteryear, i.e. the 'right' loco on the 'right' line with the 'right' stock, be it passenger or freight. Eastern European countries are favourite destinations. In communist days, I never managed more than a couple of visits to East Germany and one to Poland. SLST trips have therefore provided the opportunity to sample what it had been like in other places behind the Iron Curtain. Class 498 was a 4–8–2 express passenger design of which forty-two locos were built by Skoda in 1946/7. Painted light blue with red wheels and frames, they were most visually impressive machines. No. 498.022 is photographed near Porin, Czech Republic, with a SLST special in October 2002.

In Hungary in April 2001, no. 424.009 approaches Leanyvar with a SLST special from Dorog to Budapest. Construction of this 4–8–0 class for the Hungarian state railways started in 1924 and continued until 1958. A later model appears in the chapter on freight trains.

Re-creation of a steam era branch line, near Epleny, Hungary, in May 2001. No. 375.562 is the only active survivor of a class of Prairie tanks comprising 700 locos built over a fifty-year period.

Germany was a prodigious manufacturer of steam locos. Between 1942 and 1945 more than 6,000 *kriegslokomotiven* (war locomotives) were built. With a 2–10–0 wheel arrangement, the class was designed for quickness and economy of construction, and for ease of maintenance. After the war examples were to be found throughout those parts of Europe which had been occupied by the Nazis. One such loco, now numbered 33.037, exits a tunnel near Bled, Slovenia, with a RTC special in June 2008.

Opposite: The Czech Republic, too, offers the authentic branch scene. No. 310.093 crosses Holubovsky viaduct near Kremze with a charter train from Ceske Budejovice to Cesky Krumlov in October 2002. With a 0–6–0 wheel arrangement, she was built in Prague in 1901.

The ex-Prussian 4–6–0 P8 was another class which strayed over much of Europe thanks to German occupation in the Second World War. This example is now preserved in Austria, though originating from Romania, and carries the number 638.1301. The low angle of the late afternoon sun is perfect for illuminating the wheels in this shot taken near Ampflwang, Austria, in October 2004.

Hungary can even provide an authentic nineteenth-century train. No. 269 is an 0–6–0, one of a class of some 150 locos built between 1869 and 1878. She puts on a good show for the SLST photographers alongside the River Danube at Nyergesujfalu in May 2001.

However, the environment isn't always authentic. No. 204 arrives at Labatlan, Hungary, in May 2001. The incongruous juxtaposition of train and background appealed to me but there's no chance of this scene being described as 'timeless' – an adjective so beloved of magazine editors but so mistakenly used.

In Jordan, no. 71 looks absolutely right as she threads through the suburbs of Amman in September 2008. Details of her origins can be found in a later chapter.

5

Freight Trains

As in the previous chapter, let's have the real thing to start with, and where better than China? With independent travel now possible pretty well everywhere, excepting sensitive areas such as military zones, it's easy to forget the restrictions and frustrations facing gricers not that many years ago. When I first went to China in 1982, the solo traveller was almost unknown. Western visitors went in groups with official guides and much of the country was off-limits. There was steam in large quantity, much more in fact than was realised at the time, but access to it was at best difficult and at worst impossible. Perversely, one place tourists were allowed to visit was the factory at Datong where steam locos were still being built. Gradually more and more of the country became accessible allowing the 'discovery' of some very 'steamy' places. One of these was Yebaishou, in Liaoning Province north-east of Beijing, where three busy secondary routes converged. Opened to Westerners in the mid-1990s, it quickly became well known to the gricing community. All three routes had to climb out of Yebaishou, thus offering plenty of locations for photographing steam hard at work. On the route to Chifeng, a double-headed freight approaches the tunnel between Shina and Shahai in November 1996.

The vantage point used for the previous photograph offered an unusual view of the leading loco. All the engines seen at Yebaishou were Class QJ 2–10–2s. Introduced in 1957, locos of this class continued to be constructed at Datong until the late 1980s. Numbering over 7,000, they became the mainstay of latter-day steam on the Chinese national network. QJ? Steam loco classes in China were, obviously, denoted in Chinese characters. Phonetically, the characters for this class are Qian Jin which roughly translates as 'progress'. Other steam classes included JF 'liberation', JS 'construction' and SY 'aim high'.

The star turn on the Yebaishou to Chifeng route was the morning coal train from Pingzhuang, seen here approaching the summit of the line from the north in November 1996. The sight and sound were literally awesome, although in the excitement I forgot to record the numbers of the locos.

Opposite: Next day, the train was photographed from the other side of the line. There's obviously maximum effort as there really are two QJs here.

Some freights were short enough to require only one loco. No. 6709 (or is that 6708?) climbs away from Shina in November 1996.

The last shot of the day near Shina in November 1996.

The line from Yebaishou towards Fuxin and Shenyang reached a summit between Gongzingzi and Bolouchi. A tender-to-tender double-headed freight approaches the top from the east in November 1996. The leading QJ no. 3185 is blowing-down, the process for forcing out the sludge which settles at the bottom of the boiler.

Tender-first locos aren't very photogenic, so one needs to be creative to make an interesting shot like this one near Bolouchi, China, in November 1996.

At about the same time as Yebaishou was being 'discovered', a brand new steam-worked mainline opened running 600 miles east–west across the Inner Mongolia Autonomous Region. Known as the JiTong railway, it soon became *the* place where everyone wanted to go, until steam was finally replaced by diesels in 2005. The most-visited locations were around the Jingpeng Pass, a 30-mile section of line with tunnels, horseshoe curves, spectacular viaducts, steep gradients – in short, the lot. Such was the topography that from some vantage points it was possible to watch the same train for almost an hour. Many of the best spots required a deal of walking to reach. One which didn't was the eastern end of the summit tunnel. QJ no. 6735 leads a double-headed train of timber, the last wagon of which is out of sight beyond the left-hand edge of this photograph, near Shangdian, China, in March 2004.

Another lazy location was the level crossing in the middle of the 180 degree curve at San Di, on the eastern side of the pass, seen here in sun in October 1997 . . .

. . . and in snow in March 2004.

Hainan Island, off China's southern coast, is a world away from Inner Mongolia. The town of Basou on the west of the island is well within the tropics. In 1996, steam-worked trains of iron ore ran from the mines at Shiliu to Basou docks. Class JF 2–8–2s were once found on secondary routes all over China. By the mid-1990s, Hainan Island was one of their last stamping grounds. An unidentified member of the class runs back into the main station at Basou with a train of empties from the docks in November 1996. This photograph took at lot of patience and when the train eventually appeared, careful timing of the shutter was required.

Poland was the last country in Europe to see regular steam-hauled freights on the standard gauge. Class Ty45 2–10–0 no. 20 shunts at Konotop prior to picking-up a few timber wagons to take to Wolsztyn in April 2000.

Specialist overseas tours sometimes give the chance to photograph period freights. 'Mixeds' would be a more accurate description of these because there is usually a coach hooked on the back. One such mixed headed by Class 19D no. 2698 is seen at Pretoriuskloof, South Africa, in July 1995.

The same train on the last stages of the southern climb to the Lootsberg Pass, South Africa, in July 1995.

A mixed enters the gorge at Jagpoort on the northern side of the Lootsberg Pass, South Africa, in July 1995. Class 19D nos 2698 and 3324 head and bank the train respectively.

Class 15A *Milly* was for many years the station pilot at De Aar, one of the last steam strongholds on South African Railways. She was a 4–8–2 built by Beyer Peacock in 1921 and is seen here leaving Simonstown with a charter mixed bound for Cape Town in July 1995.

Somewhat more substantial power was provided for this mixed in the shape of Class GO Garratt no. 2575 at Mission on the line from Caledon to Cape Town, South Africa, in July 1995.

Another example of power overkill as Class 24 no. 3635 *Rika* and Class 19D no. 2698 climb out of Elliot, South Africa, in July 1995.

In South Africa's winter, there's frost on the ground as Class 19D no. 2698 struggles to keep its footing shortly after leaving Indwe with a charter mixed bound for Sterkstrom in July 1995.

As dusk approaches, the same train runs through Glen Wallace in July 1995.

In Ukraine, a charter freight arrives at Yaremtcha in September 1994. The leading loco is a Class Er 0–10–0 no. 770-99; the other Class Te 2–10–0 no. 5653. There are interesting stories to both classes. Class E dates from Czarist Russia, the first loco emerging from the workshops in 1912. After the Revolution, the Soviet railways adopted and adapted the design as one of its standard classes for shunting, freight and light passenger duties, and continued to build new locos in great quantities. Indeed, after the ravages of the Second World War, large numbers of derivatives of the class were built and supplied to the USSR by other Eastern Bloc countries. Exact figures are not known but it is thought that the total number of locos of Class E and its spin-offs might have been as high as 13,500 making it by far the largest steam class-group in the world. As its army advanced eastwards in 1941, Germany deployed well over a thousand *kriegslokomotiven* on the Russian front, some of which were built to the Russian gauge of 5ft. When the tide turned later in the war, many were captured by the Red Army. In effect, they became war booty, *trofiya* in Russian, hence Class T.

Opposite top: Later in its journey, the train seen in the previous photograph approaches Vorohkta. No. 5653 is almost dwarfed by the leading loco, emphasising the more generous height of the Russian loading gauge compared with the German.

Opposite bottom: This locomotive is of the same class as no. 424.009 seen in the chapter on passenger trains, though one would never guess so from appearances. In age, thirty years separate them. No. 424.247 has many different features including a double chimney and smoke deflectors, and of course a prominent Red Star. She puts on smoke for the photographers as she nears Hatvan, Hungary, with a Steam Loco Safari Tours charter freight in May 2001.

No. 424.247 makes a fine sight departing from Nagybatony, Hungary, in May 2001.

2–6–2 no. 324.540 was constructed in Budapest in 1915, one of a class of over 900 locos built between 1909 and the early 1940s. She works a SLST charter mixed seen shortly after leaving Zirc, Hungary, in May 2001.

Finally in this chapter, something a little different – and on a museum line. Where the narrow gauge connected with the standard gauge, it was necessary for freight consignments from one to the other to be manhandled. To avoid this, transporter wagons were sometimes used. They consisted of a narrow gauge base on which a standard gauge wagon could be carried in piggy-back style. 0–10–0 no. 99 1715–4 approaches Schmalzgrube with a demonstration freight on the preserved Pressnitztalbahn, Germany, in October 2004.

6

Signals, Signs and Such Like

This gantry has lost some of its signals and all the finials are missing. Even so, it looks impressive as Class YC Pacific no. 629 leaves Bago, Burma, on a train for Mandalay in January 2007, a journey of 340 miles which occupied nigh on forty hours. Such jaunts require stamina as well as dedication.

In countries which were once part of the Empire, the British influence in railway design is still much in evidence as at Bago, Burma. Class YD 2–8–2 no. 970 puts on a show for photographers with a Railway Touring Company special in January 2007.

The British influence was not confined to the Empire. In parts of South America, British capital and British engineering were responsible for much of the rail network. This fine pair of signals, reminiscent of those on my childhood clockwork train layout, was in Uruguay. 2–6–0 no. 120 is a British product having been built in Manchester by the firm of Beyer Peacock in 1910. She is seen heading an enthusiasts' excursion from Montevideo to Florida – no, not the US state – in December 1992. Apparently, the loco is actually no. 119, having had a number swap at some time.

There's a certain type of gricer who needs to identify and record the precise details of every locomotive seen, dead or alive. To such enthusiasts, makers' plates are an invaluable source of information. Here's a trio from British manufacturers but I'll leave those in the know to work out to which locos they belong.

New Zealand, October 1991.

Isle of Man, April 1996.

The ex-German war locomotive bearing this plate was still at work in Serbia in June 2008.

The builder's plate of Ybbstalbahn no. 598.02 featured in the narrow gauge chapter. It is photographed here in October 2004.

Caked with grease and coal dust, this plate adorned one of the powerful Japanese-built 2–10–2s on the 75cm gauge line linking coal mines at Rio Turbio with the port of Rio Gallegos, Argentina. It is seen in December 1992.

Above left: The cabsides of Polish steam locomotives carry a set of three plates. The topmost depicts the state emblem and the initials of the railway administration, while the middle and lowest denote the class and number of the loco respectively. In this instance, there is also a warning about overhead electric wires, and a plaque of the Virgin Mary and Child. One of the volunteer drivers at Wolsztyn is about to board the loco prior to taking a passenger train to Poznan in April 2000. *Above right:* In some countries, maintenance dates appear on cabsides. No. 399.02 was working one of the regular passenger trains which at the time ran on the narrow gauge line from Gmund to Gross Gerung, Austria. I'd love to have the brass numberplate in my collection. It is photographed in September 1995.

Right: No. 71 is a 2–8–2 built for the Hedjaz-Jordan Railway in 1955 by the Belgian makers Haine St Pierre. She was seen at Amman in September 2008.

Far right: The smokebox numberplate and headlamps of no. 1571, a Class SY 2–8–2, are photographed through the open vestibule of the first carriage of a passenger train on the Tiefa Mining Administration's system, China, in February 2004.

The Chinese have a fondness for slogans. 'Harmony and safety' is the message displayed on SY no. 400. She is being re-coaled and re-watered on the railway system serving coal mines and pits in the Pingzhuang area in October 2007. The brass numberplate atop the smokebox was very covetable.

'Safety first – zero accidents,' proclaims the mural at the entrance to the workshops at Sandaoling, another of China's 'private' coal railways. Three days' photography here in March 2009 produced twenty active steam locos, an incredible number for the end of the first decade of the twenty-first century.

Embellishment of the cylinder casing of a loco at Jesus Rabi sugar mill, Cuba, in March 2000.

Left: Dak bungalows are used by senior officials as overnight accommodation at Pithoro Junction, Pakistan, in February 1988.

Above: Note the driver in this Chinese level crossing sign seen in October 2007.

Above: Evidence that Hungary was part of the former Eastern Bloc. The use of English seems surprising, Budapest, May 2001.

Above: Nothing to do with God's Wonderful Railway – the station at Great Western, Sri Lanka, serves a tea estate of the same name. It was photographed in February 1994.

Left: Stained glass at Dunedin railway station, New Zealand, in October 1991.

7

Industrial Steam

Until the drastic reduction of sugar production, as mentioned in the next chapter, Cuba's mills provided a wealth of industrial steam. An added bonus was the tropical climate – such a pleasant change from winters in China's frozen north – and the cigars. One of the favourite systems was that serving Rafael Freyre sugar mill, located towards the eastern end of the island. Set in lush, rolling countryside, this was a lovely place to watch 2ft 6in gauge Baldwin 2–8–0s working hard on long trains of cane. Self-drive cars, available at the nearby resort of Guardalavaca on the Atlantic coast, enabled trains to be chased though one had to be prepared for a rough ride on dirt roads which were especially hazardous after rain. No. 1387 brings a full load of cane under the bridge carrying the main road to Guardalavaca across the railway in March 2000. The number on the smokebox door is the same as when the loco was originally supplied to the mill. The number 1387, as displayed on the cabside, is the Sugar Ministry number, all the mills being, of course, state-owned since the 1959 Revolution.

No. 1386 is about to pass under the same bridge in March 1995.

Near Altuna in March 2000.

Espartaco was another mill with a photogenic 2ft 6in gauge system and yet more 2–8–0 Baldwins.
Built as long ago as 1895, no. 1326 shunts wagons in the yards in March 2000.

The lines serving Obdulio Morales and Simon Bolivar mills shared the same unusual gauge of 2ft 3¾in, though the precise width of the tracks seems to have been the matter of some dispute by gricers. The two systems met at Centeno where in March 1995 no. 1354, a 2–8–0 Baldwin of 1921 vintage, works a train of empties from Obdulo Morales.

Five years later, Simon Bolivar's no. 1360, another 2–8–0 Baldwin built in 1917, works a train in the opposite direction.

Gregorio Arlee Manalich mill was an hour or so's drive from Havana. It had steam on two gauges, 2ft 6in and standard. On the narrow gauge, no. 1306, a Baldwin 2–8–0 built in 1912, was painted black in February 1995.

In March 2000 she was aquamarine.

The level crossing at the entrance to the mill yard saw frequent activity, as can be seen in this March 2000 photograph of sister loco no. 1308, which was twelve years older than no. 1306.

Cuba is famous for its ancient American automobiles, as seen at Gregorio Arlee Manalich mill in March 2000.

Pablo de la Torriente Brau mill, in the west of the island, had a small fleet of standard gauge locos. Unusually for Cuba, 2–6–0 no. 1703 was of German origin having being built by Henschel in 1920. In February 1995 she shunts the yards at the mill.

Another 2–6–0, this time from the Vulcan Iron Works, USA, brews-up outside the sheds at P T Brau in February 1995. No. 1102 was constructed in 1915.

There's no doubting the country of origin of standard gauge 2–8–0 no. 1629, seen at Antonio Sanchez mill in March 1995. She was built by the American Locomotive Company in 1920.

Opposite top: Standard gauge no. 1515 of Australia mill will be seen again in the next chapter. Here she brings a loaded train across Cuba's only motorway in March 1995. No gates? Just a lady with a flag? Not a problem, as the only vehicle to be seen is a bicycle. A fruit vendor is trading from a cart in the central reservation.

Opposite bottom: No. 1343 shunts the yards at Marcelo Salado mill in March 1995, another standard gauge operation. She was a 2–6–2 saddle tank constructed by Baldwin in 1904.

More Baldwin 2–8–0s, again on the standard gauge. No. 1807 shunts loaded wagons at Juan Avila mill in March 1995 . . .

Opposite: . . . and no. 1804 heads a full load of cane towards Amistad con los Pueblos mill in March 2000.

Well into the twenty-first century, China had a goodly number of industrial locations which used steam locos. Baiyin lies to the north of the city of Lanzhou in Gansu Province. It has a 'private' rail network linking mines with factories where copper, lead and zinc are smelted. In March 2009, SY no. 1047 works hard against the grade with a rake of empties for the mines at Shenbutong. The wonders of digital technology have helped create this picture because, as the train approached the vantage point, a succession of shots was taken, but unfortunately the final frame did not include the whole train, a defect which has been remedied by merging it with the previous frame.

No. 1581 looks superb in the early morning light as she heads towards Shenbutong with the train seen in the previous photograph – truly a sight to gladden the heart.

Pingdingshan in central China is the centre of an extensive coal-mining area with its own railway system which too has its own passenger trains. In October 2007 these were still steam-hauled and JS no. 5644 leaves the main station with an afternoon departure. As in many industrial locations in China, air pollution was a particular problem for photography at Pingdingshan, so the sun's appearance was as welcome as it was rare.

Opposite, bottom: The Baiyin Company runs a passenger service for its workers. The morning train to Shenbutong approaches Dongchanggau Halt with SY no. 1581 in charge in March 2009. No digital manipulation has been required this time because all of the visible carriages were captured – just. In fact, this train had six coaches but the last two are out of sight in the curved cutting to the rear.

Jixi, in the north-east of China, not far from the border with Russia, is the centre of an extensive coal-mining area with a number of 'private' rail systems connected to the national network. That at Chengzihe is one of the busiest and at the time of my visits in March and November 2009 was 100 per cent steam. There are plans to electrify the system. Indeed, a batch of second-hand electric locos has been acquired. However, the news at the time of writing seems to be that the economic climate and the prospect of unemployment among steam loco crews have put paid to these plans, though presumably only temporarily. So if industrial steam is your thing, go now; don't wait for a group tour. Plan your own itinerary, hire a guide and driver – you won't find yourself sleeping in luxury accommodation but you'll certainly experience local life. After all, where else would one be offered chicken claws or donkey meat for dinner? Meanwhile, in March 2009 a train of coal from the Chengzihe system hauled by a SY approaches the exchange yards at Jixi Xi. This part of China is notorious for its cold winters. Even with six layers of clothes, it still felt perishing. At four o'clock in the afternoon and with the light fading, it was time to retreat to the Northern Territory Resources Mansion hotel for a hot bath – and a beer or three.

Opposite top and bottom: The steeply-graded steelworks line at Chengde was much photographed in its day. Up trains often needed three locos, though only two were required for this coal-train in October 1997. SY no. 872 is at the front while an unidentified JS banks at the rear.

The washery at Beichang as seen in March 2009. A footbridge out of sight to the right was a super vantage point for watching the constant comings and goings. Although in a very different setting, it was reminiscent of a childhood haunt – the bridge over the tracks and yards to the west of the station at Taunton, Somerset. Known as Forty Steps, it's still there today.

Opposite: Elsewhere on the Chengzihe system, another SY works a train of coal from Dongchang mine to Beichang washery in March 2009.

Didao is another of the 'private' systems in the Jixi area. Here too, traffic is heavy and includes workings to and from a local power station. Sadly from a photographic point of view, the driver of this SY, on a rake of empties, shut off steam just before the picture was taken in March 2009.

SY no. 0407 has just brought a rake of loaded wagons into a local coal yard at Didao in March 2009. The late afternoon sun provides perfect illumination.

Coal and snow are well suited to black and white photography. Perhaps this shot, taken in Didao, Jixi, in November 2009, conveys something of the bleakness of the mining environment in winter.

One of the less frequently visited Chinese colliery systems is at Beipiao in Liaoning Province. With only six SYs, it's a fairly small-scale operation though there always seems to be something going on at the washery and there are definitely no diesels in this November 2009 view. Don't look at the proliferation of wires and the unsightly floodlight pylon. Savour the atmosphere of a steam-worked coal railway at first light.

Opposite: By October 2007 the once ubiquitous QJs had almost disappeared, even from industrial systems to which they had been relegated, as steam was eliminated from the national network. Two survived on the Yankuang Coal Railway where, with luck, they could be found hauling huge loads of coal to the local power stations. Was this the last place in China to see QJs in full cry?

Light engines generally don't make interesting photographs, but as the smoke effects (above) had been created for our benefit, it seemed rude not press the shutter. Unusually for a QJ, no. 7126 (below left) had high smoke deflectors instead of the more usual design carried by no. 7189 (above and below right). Spread throughout the trains of coal wagons were armed guards whose purpose was presumably to prevent pilfering. From their obviously friendly waves, it seemed they weren't there to apprehend gricers.

Anshan steelworks covers a vast area and has its own extensive rail system. The management had a very relaxed attitude towards gricers. On paying an entry fee, visitors were given a hard hat and a warning to be careful, and that was that. One could wander at will around the area occupied by the blast furnaces, outside of which there was a constant coming and going of steam locos hauling the huge cauldrons used for taking molten slag to the tips. However, the heavy pollution in the atmosphere made photography somewhat iffy at times. Here, in October 1997, SY no. 0573 sets off for the tips . . .

. . . while no. 0429 waits to back onto the next load.

The Dahuichang limestone narrow gauge railway was on the outskirts of Beijing. Its purpose was to take stone from a quarry to a crushing plant from where it was transferred to the standard gauge. In March 2004, a train of empties approaches the quarry while a loaded train disappears in the distance. This industrial concern has since ceased operations.

In November 2009 SY no. 1118, sporting a red star, leaves the loading point at Pinggang colliery near Jixi with a full load of coal. At the time of my visit to China in 1982, the first of eight over the years, there were thought to be as many as 10,000 steam locos at work and new ones were still being built. How things have changed. Nevertheless, be amazed not at what has disappeared but at what remains. At the end of the first decade of the twenty-first century, there's nowhere else in the world where everyday steam can be found in quantity. Two trips to China in 2009 produced 88 active steam locomotives at seven locations. Who says real steam is dead?

A change of continent – Europe. In 2008 a number of coal mines in Bosnia-Herzegovina still used steam locos. That at Banovici did so on two gauges, 76cm and standard. After the Second World War, Yugoslavia acquired a number of 0–6–0 tanks built in the USA. This class saw service in many parts of Europe, including England. So pleased were the Yugoslav authorities with their locos that more were built locally in the 1950s, including no. 62-125, seen here shunting on the standard gauge in June 2008.

Finally in this chapter, a museum operation – the Muskau Forestry Railway in what was East Germany. This 60cm system operated from 1896 until 1978. It was later rescued by enthusiasts and reconstructed to a high standard of authenticity. Locos include this 0–8–0 tank built for the railway in 1918 and photographed in October 2004.

8

Locomotive Sheds

Steam sheds are special places and have a unique atmosphere. For me, it's the aroma – a warm blend of smoke, steam, oil and grease. Night time adds a dash of mystery and here, surely, this April 1994 photograph shows steam's high altar. My first visit to Poland was in the mid-1970s when the country was a very steamy place on both standard and narrow gauges. Twenty years later it was a different scene with only a handful of outposts of active steam. One of these was Wolsztyn in the west of the country. Five secondary routes converged there. The depot provided steam locos for freights and, on three of the routes, passenger trains. When in 1994 *Steam Railway* magazine advertised a 48-hour trip, I knew I just had to go to see what by then was, I think, the last standard gauge daily steam operation in Europe on a national system. A charter flight and coach journey got us to Wolsztyn before dawn in time for a spot of night photography at the sheds under a full moon.

Fast forward six years and, unbelievably, there was I driving passenger and freight trains covering 600 miles in a week. (The how and why are explained in the chapter on stations.) After arriving with a train from Wolsztyn in April 2000, Class Ol49 no. 69 ran light engine to the sheds at Poznan to be cleaned, watered and turned. Positioning the loco on the turntable was a job for the regular crew. I did help with the cleaning, though it looks as if we didn't have time to do the tender before heading back onto our train for the return journey. When I came here in 1975, these sheds were full of steam locos.

Not all turntables see such regular use as that at Poznan. It took a lot of effort to move the one at Kocevlje, Slovenia, in June 2008.

The atmosphere is almost tangible at Catalagzi, Turkey, in April 1984 . . .

. . . and Jalainur, in China's far north. This place was famous among the gricing fraternity because of its huge open-cast coal mine. All day long and all night too, trains zig-zagged down into, and up out of, the pit. It was an amazing operation without a diesel in sight. In October 2007, two and a half days' photography produced 35 active steam locos.

Sunlight slants through the smoke in the shed-come-works at Baiyin, China, in March 2009. If only one could bottle the aroma!

No. 2458 is an 0–6–0 of a classic British design. Built by the Vulcan Foundry in 1920, she emerges from the sheds at Rawalpindi, Pakistan, in February 1988. By then, she saw infrequent use as shed pilot, diesels having taken over all train work from the depot the previous year.

Lala Musa, Pakistan, in February 1988. It's a shame that the reflection is not quite dead-centre.

The attractions of Cuba as a steam destination have already been remarked upon. Though banished from the country's main railways, steam flourished for a few months each year at those sugar mills which had rail connections to the cane fields. The peak period was February to April, the time of the *zafra* (sugar harvest). Over 100 mills were recorded as using steam locos at one time or another, on four different gauges and of a variety of types. The vast majority of the engines were American having been acquired well before the 1959 Revolution. The country's subsequent lack of foreign exchange coupled with the US trade embargo meant it was well nigh impossible to buy new locos to replace the ageing sugar fleet. So, as with the vintage cars on Havana's streets, it was a case of make do and mend; and it was a tribute to local skill and ingenuity that so many locos were still at work at the beginning of the twenty-first century. That situation, however, didn't last. A change of policy by the Cuban government to develop tourism rather than sugar as the main source of foreign exchange meant the closure of a huge number of mills. As a result, 2009 reports indicated active steam locos at just a couple of mills. No. 1827 was a standard gauge 2–8–0 Baldwin built in 1920, and is seen outside the sheds at Ciro Redondo mill in March 2000.

Three of the locos on the narrow gauge system serving the Simon Bolivar mill rest outside the sheds in March 1995.

It's not so much a shed as a servicing point at the Jose Smith Gomas mill. No. 1122 was an 0–4–0 built at the Porter Locomotive Works, Pittsburgh, USA, in 1909 and is seen here in February 1995. Note the pony and trap, a common sight in Cuba.

No. 1808 was a Baldwin 2–6–0 of 1927 vintage. She raises steam outside the sheds at Cuba Libre mill in March 1995 – just look at that smoke! Wow!

Another servicing point, this time at Australia mill, seen in March 1995. No. 1515 was a 4–6–0 supplied by the American Locomotive Company in 1914 to the then Havana Central Railroad. I failed to record details of the other engine.

The sheds and works of the metre gauge Dona Teresa Cristina railway at Tubarao, Brazil, in November 1981 – a glamorous name in stark contrast to the line's function as a coal-carrier. Bought second-hand from Argentina to which they had been supplied new by Skoda in 1949, 2–10–2s nos 400 and 401 had had a truly international career.

Two QJs at Daban, China, in October 2007.

Another pair of locos, this time outside the small depot at Deraa, Syria, in September 2008.

The time to visit the sheds at Bulawayo, Zimbabwe, was at first light when locos were being prepared for their day's work. This photograph from July 1989 demonstrates how the plethora of wires, poles and other bits of ironmongery at loco depots does little to assist pictorial composition. As it was, I had to wait for the sun to be sufficiently high in the sky to light the wheels and motion of the nearest loco. Fortunately there was plenty of smoke to add to the atmosphere. Wonderful. No. 741 is a Class 20A Garratt with a 4–8–2 + 2–8–4 wheel arrangement built by Beyer Peacock in 1957. The other two locos are smaller 2–6–2 + 2–6–2 Class 14A Garratts used mainly for shunting and short-haul freights.

Minor repairs at Varanasi, India, in November 1985.

In the workshops at Ceske Velenice, Czech Republic, in October 2002 where steam locomotives were still being overhauled.

Outside the workshops at Anshan steelworks, China, in November 1996.

The workshops of the railways which serve the Kreka coalmines near Tuzla in Bosnia-Herzegovina are at Bukinje. In the yard is a memorial to those railway staff killed in the fighting in that part of the world between 1992 and 1996. It is photographed in June 2008.

Light catches the smokebox of Class JS no. 6509 in the sheds at Basuo, Hainan Island, China, in November 1996.

What happened here? Some sort of explosion appears to have wrecked the cab of this loco at Australia sugar mill, Cuba, in March 2000.

The sheds at either end of the narrow gauge line from Radebeul (above) to Radeburg (below) in Germany, seen in April 2002. The loco is one of a large class of 2–10–2 tanks built before and after the Second World War. No. 99 1778-2 is from a post-war batch built in what was then East Germany at the aptly named Karl Marx Works.

Contrasts in coaling. With steam-powered cranes in bitterly cold weather at Daban, China, in March 2004 (above), it's a case of doing it by hand in the rain at Chvalkov, Czech Republic, in October 2004 (below).

There's a lot of muck in and around engine sheds and they're certainly no place for anyone with a cleanliness fetish. At Islampur, India, ash is being cleaned from the smokebox in November 1985.

The environs of Cadem works, Damascus, Syria, have a general air of untidiness in September 2008.

And so to bed! The 7th class of the Cape Government Railways in South Africa was introduced in the 1890s. With a 4–8–0 wheel arrangement, the class was intended for freight traffic and two survived into the 1980s to work on colliery railways. No. 1007 was later restored for mainline running in which condition she is photographed at George, South Africa, in July 1995.

THE END

China, November 1996.